Sybil Ludington's MIDNIGHT RIDE

by Marsha Amstel
illustrations by Ellen Beier

Carolrhoda Books, Inc./Minneapolis

For Morty, Robyn, and David, with gratitude and love
—M. A.

For Stuart
  —E. B.

The artist would like to thank Kathleen Zuris of the Danbury Scott-Fanton Museum and Historical Society and Richard Muscarella, Putnam County Historian, for their assistance.

Text copyright © 2000 by Marsha Amstel
Illustrations copyright © 2000 by Ellen Beier

This book is available in two editions:
Library binding by Carolrhoda Books, Inc.,
   a division of Lerner Publishing Group
Soft cover by First Avenue Editions,
   an imprint of Lerner Publishing Group
241 First Avenue North
Minneapolis, MN 55401 U.S.A.

Website address: www.lernerbooks.com

Library of Congress Cataloging-in-Publication Data

Amstel, Marsha.
   Sybil Ludington's midnight ride / by Marsha Amstel ; illustrations
by Ellen Beier.
      p.   cm. — (Carolrhoda on my own books)
   Includes index.
   Summary: The story of Sybil Ludington's ride on horseback to rouse
American soldiers to fight against the British who were attacking
Danbury, Connecticut during the American Revolution.
   ISBN 1-57505-211-3 (lib. bdg. : alk. paper)
   ISBN 1-57505-456-6 (pbk. : alk. paper)
   1. Ludington, Sybil, b. 1761—Juvenile literature. 2. Danbury
(Conn.)—History—Burning by the British, 1777—Juvenile literature.
3. United States—History—Revolution, 1775–1783—Biography—
Juvenile literature. 4. United States—History—Revolution,
1775–1783—Women—Juvenile literature. [1. Ludington, Sybil,
b. 1761 2. Danbury (Conn.)—History—Burning by the British, 1777.
3. United States—History—Revolution, 1775–1783—Biography.
4. Women—Biography.] I. Beier, Ellen, ill. II. Title. III. Series.
E241.D2A47 2000
973.3'33—dc21   98-44155

Manufactured in the United States of America
2 3 4 5 6 7 – JR – 06 05 04 03 02 01

Author's Note

History is not always fair. Some stories are remembered and repeated. Others are forgotten. Sometimes, history remembers his story and forgets hers.

In 1775, most Americans had become impatient with being a colony of Great Britain. They wanted their own government. They wanted to make laws and solve problems on their own. They wanted to be a free and independent nation. But Great Britain had no intention of letting its colony go free.

Many British soldiers came on ships to Boston. Americans began to prepare for war. On April 18, Paul Revere rode through the countryside warning everyone, "The British are coming! The British are coming!" The next day, Americans fought with British soldiers at the Battle of Lexington. This was the beginning of the Revolutionary War.

Two years later, America was still at war. Henry Ludington, a farmer and mill owner in Patterson, New York, had been chosen by General George Washington to be the leader of 400 soldiers. After months of fighting, Colonel Ludington and his men were given permission to return to their farms so that they could plant their spring crops. On April 26, 1777, the soldiers were at home with their families.

That Saturday evening, Colonel Ludington learned that British troops had attacked his neighbors in Danbury, Connecticut. He needed someone who could round up his soldiers quickly, so they could march to Connecticut and stop the British. It was a dangerous and difficult mission. Colonel Ludington needed someone who was brave and determined.

This is the story of Sybil Ludington's midnight ride. It is a true story.

April 26, 1777
Patterson, New York

The night began with the sounds
of hoofbeats and shouting.
The noises surprised
the whole Ludington family.
There were no neighbors close by.
Who could be visiting
on such a cold, rainy night?

Sybil Ludington was 16 years old.
She was the oldest
of eight brothers and sisters.
Sybil worked hard helping her mother
take care of the younger children.
She helped with spinning and knitting
and weaving and sewing.
She gardened and cooked and baked.
She made soap and candles and butter.
Everything the family needed
was made right at home.

When Sybil had finished her chores,
she loved to go riding on Star.
Star was a big horse with a white patch
in the middle of his forehead.
The shape of the patch gave him his name.

Star was just one year old,
not yet fully grown.
Sybil had trained him herself.
She loved to gallop through the fields
with the wind in her face
and her hair flying out behind her.

On that rainy night in April, everyone
in the Ludington house was very happy.
Sybil's father had just returned home
for a visit.
A big bright fire crackled in the fireplace.
Colonel Henry Ludington was telling a story
to his older children.

Sybil's mother, Abigail, and her sister
Rebecca cleaned away the supper dishes.
Sybil was getting the littler ones
ready for bed.
Everyone stopped and stared
at the front door as hoofbeats came
to a sudden stop in the yard.

Colonel Ludington got up
to answer the knocking.
A messenger stood in the doorway.
His uniform was soaked with rain.
He shivered with cold.
He had come to tell Colonel Ludington
that 2,000 British soldiers had attacked
the town of Danbury, Connecticut.
The British were burning warehouses
filled with food and clothing
for American soldiers.
They were setting fire to Danbury homes.
There were no American soldiers
near Danbury to protect the town.

General George Washington and his army
were in Peekskill, New York.
But Peekskill was a two-day march
from Danbury.
Colonel Ludington was only
half a day away,
but his soldiers were home on their farms.
The farms were spread out
over 40 miles of countryside.

Someone would have to ride
through the night to call the men to action.
But who should go?
Colonel Ludington must stay at home
to give orders to his soldiers
as they gathered.
"I'll go," said the messenger.
But everyone could see that he was
too cold, too wet, and too tired.

"No," said Sybil. "I'll go."

"It's much too dangerous," said her mother.

"The night is cold and wet and dark.

You'll get lost in the woods."

"I can ride as well as anyone," said Sybil.

"And I know where

all Father's soldiers live."

"There might be British soldiers out there,"

said her mother.

"Worse still, the woods are full of outlaws."

"Mother," said Sybil,

"there is no one else who can go."

"The child is right," said her father.

"There is no one else."

Her mother had to agree.

Colonel Ludington went to saddle up Star.

Mrs. Ludington got her warm woolen cloak.

She wrapped it around her daughter.

Sybil picked up a big stick.

She would use it to knock on doors

to wake up sleeping families.

If she had to, she would use it

to keep away outlaws.

"Don't worry," said Sybil.

"I'll be fine."

She sounded much braver than she felt.

Sybil mounted Star.

She urged the horse into a gallop
down the dirt road.

Soon she could no longer see the lights
from her house.

Sybil had never been away from home
by herself after dark.

There was no moon out that night.

Clouds blocked the light of the stars.

By daylight, Sybil knew all the forests
and fields.

But in the dark of night,
the land was full of mysterious shapes
and strange shadows.

Sybil was surprised by how lonely she felt.

The rain was steady and hard.

Only a mile from home, raindrops started to seep through Sybil's cloak.

Her hair was soaked.

Rain ran down her face.

Then Sybil saw a flicker of candlelight through the darkness.

It was the first farmhouse on her route.

She slowed Star to a trot
and banged on the door with her stick.
"The British are burning Danbury!"
she shouted.
"Meet at Colonel Ludington's house!"
Then she urged Star on,
back into the dark woods.
She had no time to waste.

Sybil stopped at house after house.
She stayed just long enough to call out
her message and listen for an answer.
Then she would ride on into the night.
The cold rain made Sybil's teeth chatter.
Her fingers felt stiff on the reins.
She woke so many families
that she lost count.

As she rode toward the village of Carmel,
she saw a strange orange glow
in the eastern sky.
It was the light from the fires of Danbury,
20 miles away.
Sybil thought about how she would feel
if her own home were burning.
"We must hurry, Star," she whispered.

Sybil knew that she did not have to knock
at every door.

Neighbors would run to tell one another.

They would make sure that all the soldiers
heard the news.

Sybil rode into Carmel,
calling out her message.

Doors flew open at the sound of her shouts.

As she rode away,
the bell on the meetinghouse rang out.

The bell would wake the townspeople
and call them to action.

Sybil swung Star west
toward Mahopac Pond.
Here there were long, dark distances
between the farmhouses.
The narrow paths in the woods
were hard to follow.
Sometimes, Sybil had to get down
and lead Star to find their way.

Just a few weeks earlier,
the ground had been covered with snow.
But with the spring thaw and the days
of rain, there was mud everywhere.
The mud seemed to grab at Sybil's boots.
Her stockings were wet.
Her toes ached with cold.

Old, slippery leaves
covered the forest floor.
A few times, Star tripped
and Sybil almost tumbled to the ground.
But she kept going.
She had to help save Danbury.
It was early spring,
and the trees were still bare.
The branches of the big oaks and maples
stretched into the night sky.
Like giant sticks,
they waved in the wind and the rain.
Sometimes, the branches rubbed together.
They made a creaky, ghost-like noise.
Sybil closed her eyes and thought
of the new leaves of spring,
only a week or two away.

Her muscles ached.

Her throat was sore from shouting.

She thought of the warm fire

she had left behind at home.

She wished for a cup of tea

and for the sound of her mother's voice.

Sybil patted Star's neck.

She told him over and over again

what a good horse he was.

Whispering to Star made Sybil feel better.

It was hard to stay brave.

Every time a deer leaped through

the woods or an owl hooted from a tree,

Sybil's heart would pound.

Was it British soldiers?

Could it be outlaws?

Sybil took a deep breath to calm herself.

She wrinkled her nose at the sharp smells

of mud and wet leaves and wet clothes

and wet horse.

She was sure that those smells

would always remind her

of this midnight ride.

Suddenly, Sybil heard the sounds
of voices and laughter.
Just ahead, three men hunched
over a small campfire.
They were cooking a rabbit.
Their clothes were ragged and torn.
They looked like they had been living
in the woods for a long time.

Sybil knew that they were outlaws.

They stole horses and cattle from both sides
and sold them to either army.

If they got their hands on Star,

Sybil would never see him again.

Luckily, Sybil saw the outlaws
before they spotted her.
She slid off Star.
Then she walked him very slowly
through the woods.
They made a big half-circle
around the campfire.

Sybil gently stroked Star's muzzle.

She whispered, "Hush, hush."

The rain and wind covered the sounds
of their steps.

Finally they were safely past
the outlaws' camp.

When Sybil reached Stormville,

she was surprised to see lights

and to hear voices.

There, people had already heard the news.

They were gathering on the village green.

Many voices cheered for Sybil,

as Star galloped on.

"Our work is done, Star," Sybil said.

She leaned over and hugged his neck.

"Bring us home."

Finally, Sybil arrived back home,
after many cold, wet miles.
This time, the faint glow in the east
was the dawn of a new day.
Four hundred soldiers had gathered
in the field in front of the Ludington house.
The fifes and drums played.
The music seemed to be welcoming
Sybil home.
Sybil slid from Star's back
into her father's arms.
She was suddenly so tired and relieved
that she started to cry.

While Sybil slept, Colonel Ludington
and his men marched toward Danbury.
They joined other American soldiers
on the way.

The Americans were badly outnumbered.

But the British were taken by surprise.

The Americans forced them back

to the ships that had brought them.

Some people think that if it wasn't
for Colonel Ludington's soldiers,
the British could have marched to Peekskill.
There they would have attacked
General Washington's army.
That would have changed the story
of the Revolutionary War.
And that could have changed the history
of the United States.

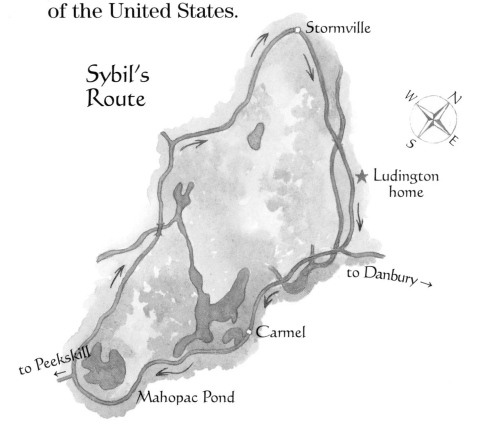

Sybil's
Route

Stormville

Ludington
home

to Danbury →

Carmel

to Peekskill

Mahopac Pond

Afterword

Almost everyone has heard about Paul Revere and his midnight ride. Yet very few people have heard of Sybil Ludington. Like Paul Revere, Sybil was patriotic and brave. Like Paul Revere, Sybil faced great danger riding through the night, warning her friends and neighbors about the British army.

Sybil Ludington rode alone, on a cold, dark, rainy night, through a forest wilderness. She rode for America's independence. Her story, and her courage, should be remembered.

After Sybil's midnight ride, George Washington came to her house to thank her. Sybil continued to work for American independence for the rest of the Revolutionary War. She helped hide Enoch Crosby, an American spy. She did guard duty to watch for the British, who were trying to capture her father.

After the war, when Sybil was 23 years old, she married Edmond Ogden. They had four sons and two daughters. She lived to be 78 years old. When she died, she was buried in a small cemetery close to the farm where she grew up.

In Carmel, New York, on the path of Sybil's midnight ride, is a wonderful, huge statue of Sybil and Star. Most statues are of famous men—usually presidents or war heroes. But Sybil Ludington was a girl, and there she is in bronze, on horseback, and bigger than life. Star is galloping through the night, while Sybil, with the wind in her face and her hair streaming wet behind her, raises her stick in the air and shouts out her message.